The

Ann Pearson is a re
Stendhal (real name .
in 1811, is *A Promise on the Horizon* (Granville Island, 2019): 'Refashioning the past in the form of episodes which ought to have happened, or almost did, is clearly Pearson's special skill, one which Monsieur Beyle himself would admire.' – Jonathan Keates, biographer of Stendhal. She has written more about Beyle on her website, www.annpearsonauthor.com.

Charles Boyle is founder-editor of CB editions. His novel about Beyle is *An Overcoat: Scenes from the Afterlife of H.B.* (CBe, 2017): 'The most innovative, intelligent, vertiginous novel to appear in years.' – Frances Wilson, *TLS*

# The Simplon Road

Two essays on Stendhal

∾

ANN PEARSON

CHARLES BOYLE

First published in Great Britain in 2023
by CB editions
146 Percy Road London W12 9QL
www.cbeditions.com

Printed in England by Imprint Digital, Exeter

ISBN 978-1-7394212-1-2

# Contents

Note on the Text

vi

Preface

vii

The Simplon Road

ix

∾

ANN PEARSON
Travelling with Beyle

1

CHARLES BOYLE
In the Provinces

41

# Note on the Text

What to call him? He whose several hundred pseudonyms mocked the whole notion of naming. Andrew Brown in his brief biography of Stendhal (Hesperus, 2010) goes for the initials of his actual name, 'HB': 'the "singular" individual behind the plurality of the pseudonyms. HB is also associated with pencils containing hard and black graphite (an allotrope of carbon named after its usefulness in writing.' Here, we have settled for Beyle.

Titles of Beyle's works in A.P.'s essay are given in their original form because she reads in French; because C.B. does not, titles in his piece are in English translation.

# Preface

More than many writers, Stendhal elicits very personal responses from his readers. Doris Lessing, returning to Stendhal/Beyle after 'a far too long interval', feels 'a rush of exhilaration, as if you have turned a corner and look! – there's an old friend you haven't seen for a time and you have forgotten what an extraordinary being he is.' The Russian writer Eduard Limonov, as related in Emmanuel Carrère's *Limonov*, loved *The Red and the Black* but while reading it was instilled with such a sense of his own wretchedness that he cut his wrist and watched his blood flow into the book before losing consciousness.

Very few readers, however, write novels about the man, and even fewer of them are English. My own was published in 2017. When I discovered that in 2019 another English writer had also published a novel about Beyle, I got in touch. The result is this slip of a book, a commentary on a joint obsession, or distraction, over decades.

Why him, and not writer X or Y or Z? Recently I asked a number of writers to name another writer who has been important to them – not necessarily the one most admired, and maybe for just a period in their lives – and the answers were sometimes predictable, sometimes surprising. One person I asked refused to name names. Perhaps out of embarrassment, perhaps because they thought I was going to steal what was *theirs*.

– C.B.

# The Simplon Road

Until 1800 nothing more than a mule-track traversed the Alps between France and Italy. It was Napoleon who saw the necessity of a road after dragging his artillery through the snows of the Great Saint-Bernard Pass to defeat the Austrians at Marengo. Lowest of the Alpine passes, the Simplon offered the most direct route between Paris and Milan, capital of the Napoleonic Kingdom of Italy (1805–14). Designed by French and Italian engineers, the road was constructed at huge expense and much cost to life and limb as thousands of workers tunnelled through rock and bridged chasms. Within five years they had produced a highway with an easily-rising gradient, wide enough for cannons or carriages to pass safely.

Napoleon never travelled the road himself, since it wasn't completed in time for his coronation as king of Italy in 1805. As events turned out, it was an Austrian army heading towards Lyon in 1815 that would profit from the road's convenience. Thus one of the emperor's greatest achievements contributed to his final defeat.

Its military importance lost, the Simplon became the favourite route to Italy for travellers from the north in the post-Waterloo tourist boom, among them the Wordsworths, Byron and the Shelleys. Henri Beyle took the Simplon road many times as he oscillated between Paris, intellectual centre of Europe, and Italy, his beloved, often maddening, but true homeland.

– A.P.

ANN PEARSON ∾ Travelling with Beyle

I discovered Stendhal at twenty-one, but forty years went by before I met Henri Beyle, whose decades of self-recording took over the space on my desk newly vacated by student essays. In fact, it wouldn't be inaccurate to say he took over my life for several years. Whatever else I'd planned to do when I stopped teaching was pushed aside by a few lines in his diary which sent me, among other places, to Milan on the old Simplon road through the Alps that Beyle had travelled so often.

On the wall above my desk is a collage of early 19th-century views and some of the Italian art he loved, such as he might have sent his friends if postcards had existed then. Below, a series of portraits fan out across the years: the smug young official of 1810, and a profile of the same period (his most flattering angle); then (after a twenty-year gap) the Consul in gold-embroidered diplomatic dress (the Légion d'Honneur on his breast small recompense for the air of resignation in his eyes); an 1839 portrait with an amused sideways glance that conveys the novelist's sharp observation and the confidence

1

of a man who's just published *La Chartreuse de Parme*; and finally a pencil drawing from 1841 (a year before his death), gamely smiling despite a first stroke. From the back row, the eyes of the tongue-tied adolescent engage mine with a mute appeal for recognition.

That's a lot of portraits (and there are more) for a man convinced he was ugly, though nothing compared to the photographic record of a modern life. Perhaps Beyle hoped a painter would capture something his mirror didn't show – what other people saw, which might just be more attractive than he thought, or that 'expressiveness' which his uncle (or his grandfather?) had told him as a boy would compensate for his ugliness? Or was it simply for the record – glimpses of the changing self he was trying to pin down in his lifelong quest for self-knowledge?

There are other writers whose lives have interested me as much as their books – Simone de Beauvoir in my twenties, Wollstonecraft much later, Woolf, Dostoevsky, John Stuart Mill. Troubled beings, most of them, Beyle too, though to a lesser degree. You have to be wary, though, in admitting to a fascination with Beyle. There's a 'club', or a 'cult', which you might not want to be identified with – the Beylistes – described by an unfriendly critic as 'a self-recruiting sect whose hero isn't merely the creator of Julien Sorel and Fabrice del Dongo but a supreme master of the art of life, the very model of the free man, and a spiritual ally in their quest for sincerity'.[1]

I don't belong to that club, having met Beyle too late in life to see him as any kind of master or role model. Most women, I suspect, reading his life history feel more pity than discipleship. Personally I'm ambivalent. I feel a deep sympathy with the child and the painfully awkward youth and a fondness for the older man who persisted through many false starts and disappointments to achieve in his final decade what he'd always felt he had it in him to create. But the Beyle I know best is the man in his twenties (a stage at which many of us had an inflated idea of ourselves) and his self-centredness can be irritating. Still, the same might be said about other writers I admire – Tolstoy, for instance – yet I haven't felt any compulsion to follow up the least detail of his life as I have with Henri Beyle. What is it (apart from the hitherto unknown world he opens up) that explains the obsession?

It has something to do with the way my instinctive attraction to Beyle the rebel, the exposer of social hypocrisy and received ideas, is challenged by his deceptiveness, which, once recognised, arouses (in this reader at least) a compulsion to discover the 'truth' (if there can be such a thing in the complexity

1. Victor Brombert, *Stendhal: Fiction and the Themes of Freedom*, 1968.

of a life). Beyle believed himself to be a truth-teller by nature: at the age of ten he'd pointed out that it wasn't the machinations of a rival lawyer that had put his father on the list of known non-supporters of the Revolution since it was a *fact* that his father did not support it. (He wasn't a tactful child: no wonder his family kept him on a close rein during the Terror.) But though he aimed at total honesty in his diary (a portrayal of the 'naked animal with all his faults') he couldn't escape the longing to be a certain kind of man and at times it led him to embellish his image. However much he scorned the self-importance of officialdom, he rather liked the fancy embroidery on the various official uniforms he wore in his life. Alongside the attractive rebel and the cold-eyed cynic is Beyle the poseur who's performing even for himself.

Some of the falsehoods arose out of necessity. Early on, the risk of the diary falling into the wrong hands made him adopt protective cover – false names for himself and others, misleading statements (put in parentheses lest he be deceived himself on rereading them in later life). Once he started writing for publication it was a natural step to fabricate an authorial persona so that neither the plagiarism nor the subversive statements of his first books would rebound on him. The first fake identity – Louis-César-Alexandre Bombet – is clearly self-parodic with its three glory-filled first names and a surname that ridicules such self-importance.[2] But 'Monsieur de Stendhal' (author of two Italian travelogues and a history of painting in Italy) is less a pseudonym than an impersonation of the man Beyle would like to be – a man of noble origins who's spent three times as long in Italy as his creator, travelled to places the latter has never seen and met people who are almost certainly invented. Sometimes, as in a fairytale, the mask adheres to the face and it's impossible to tell which is the real individual.

You learn to read Beyle sceptically – if you're using an annotated edition, that is. In leaving all his autobiographical writings to posterity, he hadn't foreseen the sleuthing of modern editors, nor the extensive documentation of his life by researchers. The 'animal's faults' have been exposed more fully than he might have liked.

When, for instance, he drew up a budget in his diary on July 27, 1810, which he estimates at 14,000 francs (including 4,000 for servants and horses, 3,440 for 'plays, books, whores'), he hadn't reckoned on the assiduity of a future MA candidate who'd devote a thesis to tracking his sources of income (only 8,900 francs at the time) and his minutest expenses.[3] With expectations of a prefecture or intendancy that

2. 'bomber le torse' = 'puff out one's chest'.
3. Lily R. Felberg, *Stendhal et la question d'argent au cours de sa vie* [Editions du Grand Chêne, 1975]. Original thesis available online.

would eventually triple his income, Beyle didn't worry about his accumulating debts. Moreover, several cryptic diary notes over the next years stating that his friend Felix Faure owes him 10,000–15,000 francs indicate a hidden income stashed with Faure which, the thesis writer suggests, may have been derived from Beyle's eight years as war-commissioner and then inspector of imperial palaces, in which positions he'd have been offered the usual 'gifts' by suppliers keen to obtain a contract. This is only speculation, of course, but how else could Beyle in 1815, unemployed and with debts of 37,000 francs (at 2,000 frs. annual interest), have given his lover Angela Pietragrua ('that sublime whore', as he'd call her later) 3,000 francs to cover a visit to Venice (a last desperate attempt to retain her affection that he immediately regretted)? But all the older Beyle admits to in his autobiography (Chapter II) are a few trivial debts; only once in his life and briefly, he says, did he owe money to his tailor. By then, of course, the big debts were long since paid off and there's no reason he should mention them, but it does seem a trifle hypocritical to say he'd *never* owed more than 400 francs.

Such financial recklessness may seem commonplace in the light of modern credit-card debt, and Beyle's expectations of a high-salaried position weren't unwarranted, given the influence of his cousin, Pierre Daru, one of Napoleon's most trusted ministers. It's not the youthful extravagance (understandable in the flamboyant society of Napoleon's Paris) that's off-putting, but the endless letters badgering his father for more money (or at least the fake guarantee of an annual income that would make him eligible for a high administrative position, a guarantee which his father reluctantly provided).[4] There are also the lies to his grandfather earlier on about the child he'd supposedly fathered (for whom the generous old man sent money, which he spent on gifts for his mistress). The young Beyle had a sense of entitlement that made him impervious to shame. It's not very attractive.

And then there's the way he writes about women – not so much the predictable language of the young buck estimating them as haveable or fuckable, but the stereotyping that's less forgivable in a man who prided himself on his psychological insight. When (at the age of fifty-three) he lines up the women he's loved according to their qualities, he writes: 'To begin with their habitual passion, vanity, two of them were countesses and one a baroness.' Really, Beyle, whose vanity is on display here? A decade earlier a friend had mocked the 'ducomanie' of his Italian

4. Napoleon liked his senior administrators to be well-heeled so they could uphold the dignity of their office without claiming expenses.

travel books which made him appear a habitué of the noblest salons. Was this title snobbery just part of the false identity behind which the author could safely risk criticism of the newly-restored Austrian regime – or the self-flattering fantasy of a provincial bourgeois? A bit of both perhaps.

Of course, the inflated self-image was a defence against the early wound inflicted by his uncle, who, thinking that the boy needed taking down a peg or two, told him he was ugly and by no means as clever as he thought himself – a cruel thing to say to a sixteen-year-old leaving home for the first time, even if it was meant for his good. No wonder young Henri was paralysed by shyness. Much later, he wrote that what he'd needed at seventeen was 'a loving soul who would have recognised my own' (Diary, September 8, 1811). But no sooner has he engaged our sympathy for that lonely boy who'd so clearly needed an *initiatrice* (one to whom, unlike the women he paid for sex, he could have opened his heart), than he loses it: 'A sensitive woman would have found me charming; she would have seen in me a Roman soul for everything not concerning love.' His sensibility, he's sure, would have held her interest for a long time. With a start in life like that, he thinks, he'd have become successful with women ('un homme à femmes'), but then perhaps he wouldn't have developed such an artistic sensibility.

The narcissism this reveals is the more disconcerting in a man who dissects the failings of friends and acquaintances quite pitilessly. Because of it he could never really believe that the women he was infatuated with didn't return his love. He might have found a devoted friend in Alexandrine Daru or Metilde Dembowski if he hadn't been so obsessed with 'having' them.

All in all, it's as well I didn't meet Henri Beyle until I was old enough to look back clear-sightedly at my own youthful self-absorption and self-deception. Besides, he surely wouldn't have appealed to me earlier. The author of those two brilliant novels I read in my final year as an undergraduate was a rotund eccentric with a face distorted by tics and grimaces and the bad habit of telling off-colour stories in polite company.

He'd decided early on that wit would compensate for his lack of physical attraction, though tongue-tied as he was in society he felt he had to rehearse his witticisms like his compliments. By his thirties, though, the repartee seems to have come more naturally and he'd acquired a reputation for cleverness. An acquaintance who appears to have known him well says Beyle had decided that since he couldn't be beau he'd be bizarre and that he'd make fun of himself before others could. His appearance particularly disappointed women, who'd anticipated a man more in keeping with his passionate novels.[5]

He would certainly have disappointed the young woman I was in 1964 for whom France represented above all *style*. I'd just returned from a year as English assistant in a school in the Basses-Pyrénées, and Suffolk (at least as it appeared on the train home from Liverpool Street) seemed irremediably dull. I was determined to go back to France as soon as possible, and (if I could find the right Frenchman) to settle there for life.[6] In my suitcase was the most elegant garment I'd owned – a classic little black dress with a bunch of cherries in the décolleté (bought in Biarritz). I'd learned to use eyeliner and back-comb my hair in the dreadful fashion of the day and (according to my pupils) to walk like a Frenchwoman. True or not, I moved through the world more easily.

Growing up Catholic in a small town hadn't made for social ease. Our convent-school uniform with the JM badge designating us pupils of Jesus and Mary got us mocked as the 'Jam and Marmalade school' by the children walking in the opposite direction to the

5. Louis Desroches, 'Souvenirs anecdotiques sur M. de Stendhal', *Revue de Paris*, 1844. *Stendhal Club*, no. 5, 1959.
6. Things took a different course when, that October, I met an exchange student doing a PhD in Philosophy. Most of my life has been spent in Vancouver on the west coast of Canada.

council primary. Taught from childhood that ours was the true faith, we felt a certain superiority when we prayed for the conversion of England at Sunday Mass, but we knew enough history to be embarrassed by the monument to the Protestant martyrs burned in the market place. As a self-conscious teenager, I dreaded the annual parish procession, which paraded the statue of the Virgin from the Convent grounds to the Catholic church with full accompaniment of bells and incense, an exotic spectacle which all the locals came out to watch.

It wasn't the only reason I felt an outsider. My step-father, after some bad luck in business, struggled to find a job and had to resort for a time to farm work which, as a farmer's son, was what he knew best. I concealed it from the new friends I was making, in particular my first serious boyfriend whose father was a company director. I was moving out into a world where I knew that what your father did might count against you, no matter how well-spoken you were. It made me a pretender, just as my schooling had by leading me to enact a piety that I never really felt.

At sixteen I'd spent the summer with a wealthy French family who owned a villa in Chamonix. Their plan was that I'd speak English to their thirteen-year-old daughter (and free her mother to play golf). But young Nicole had no intention of spoiling her summer holidays with English lessons, so I was the one who gained from the exchange, perfecting my French and learning the ways of a more sophisticated world. That experience had given me some small commonality with Beyle's Julien Sorel, tutor to the sons of the rich bourgeois Monsieur de Rênal, though Julien's calculating nature precluded any easy identification of the kind I'd felt with Elizabeth Bennett or Fanny Price.[7] I'm sure I relished Stendhal's social satire as much as Austen's, but I can't separate my first impressions of *Le Rouge et le Noir* or *La Chartreuse de Parme* from later rereadings.

I read surprisingly few novels as an undergraduate, for study or for pleasure, though I'd been an avid consumer of fiction ever since I progressed (overnight it seemed) from large-print readers to real books like *Black Beauty* and *Little Women* that strange summer when I was six and daddy had mysteriously gone to heaven to live with God. Books offered explanations for the unexplained and an escape from boredom or unhappiness that became addictive. Alongside the Victorian classics and the set books we read at school, I enjoyed historical romance in my early teens (Margaret Irwin's *Young Bess* and the like) before discovering serious histor-

7. Sartre remarked somewhere that were *Le Rouge et le Noir* to be rewritten in the 20th century the protagonist would be a young woman. It's only now in the age of #MeToo that I recognise how interestingly that would reshape the plot.

ical fiction with *War and Peace.* The one novel I do remember from university (apart from the troubling erotic charge of *Les Liaisons dangereuses*), is Simone de Beauvoir's *Les Mandarins* for its portrayal of the lives of modern women. Only two of us (both girls, needless to say) took that tutorial, given by a young woman lecturer.

What interested me most (after twelve years of daily religious indoctrination at the convent) were the classic texts of French scepticism, particularly Montaigne's Essays. In our first week as undergraduates we read Descartes, whose exercise in radical doubt both reassured and disappointed me by its automatic reinstatement of faith (even if it was a sop to the authorities who might otherwise have burned the book). But he was followed by Pascal, whose affirmation of belief in the face of the 'eternal silence of infinite space' had an appeal that Descartes' prudent orthodoxy and the unthinking allegiance of cradle Catholics lacked. Of course, I was peering into the abyss from the safety of a tourist behind a guard rail, living at a Catholic hostel run by the Sisters of Charity, still going to Sunday Mass and Confession. But my intuitions of the divine were Wordsworthian rather than theological and eventually I sloughed off Catholicism as easily as my old school uniform, though the loss of belief in a benevolent Father was more painful, until one day in my final year, looking out over London from Parliament Hill Fields, I recognised the sky was empty.

A year later, in the rain of a first Vancouver autumn, I plunged into fiction. Novels were as useful as cookery books in my initiation into the middle-class world of dinner parties and faculty gatherings where the talk on one side of the room was professional, on the other domestic, and (despite Canadian friendliness) I didn't fit into either. By now I'd discovered Existentialism, which confirmed my uneasy sensation that I was always acting a part, but de Beauvoir's *Memoirs of a Dutiful Daughter* and *The Second Sex* set me to examining the script I'd been given. Not long afterwards I bought *The Golden Notebook*, *The Feminine Mystique* and *Diary of a Mad Housewife*, and found I wasn't alone in my malaise. Though I still wasn't sure what I wanted, I knew at least what I didn't want. Feeling incompetent at anything but French, I went back to university, where I discovered a whole world of French modernity that the BA curriculum had ignored. What excited me most was the exploration of consciousness in Proust and the experiments of the *nouveau roman*. After that, I scarcely looked at the classics for years (except the standard texts I was teaching), but read the new writers who were making it into the book pages.

B ut enough of all this 'I and me', as Beyle would
say. How did I meet him? What led an admirer
of the complex architecture of the Proustian sentence to an unlikely obsession with this succinct,
plain-speaking man who despised the inflated style
of his contemporaries and claimed to write with the
dry sobriety of the civil code?

It was not in a biography but in W. G. Sebald's
*Vertigo* that I first encountered Henri Beyle (alongside other travellers in Italy – Casanova, Kafka,
and the Sebaldian narrator). The book opens with
a description of Napoleon's crossing of the Alps in
1800 as experienced by the seventeen-year-old Beyle,
a junior clerk in the Ministry of War on horseback for
the first time in his life, exalted by the adventure and
still more by his first sight of Italy, a life-determining
experience as every Stendhalian knows. Sebald goes
on to describe Beyle's return to Italy after Napoleon's
fall, free at last to live the life he'd dreamed of, which
is evoked in an imagined interlude on Lake Garda
tinged with Romantic melancholy.

Curious to know just how much was fictional in
Sebald's account, I went off on a wild-goose chase
through Beyle's travel writing (and met the ultimate
unreliable narrator). But what had really gripped
me were the passages Sebald quotes from *La Vie
de Henry Brulard*. It's surely one of the most unusual autobiographies in literature, though that very

unusualness delayed its recognition, which Beyle foresaw from the start: 'To be honest I'm not at all sure I have the talent to attract readers. I sometimes get a lot of pleasure from writing, that's all.' His self-doubt isn't surprising after the reviews of *Le Rouge et le Noir* five years earlier. Reviewers, while acknowledging its originality, had been put off by a style recognised as witty but judged cold, mocking, clinical in its dissection, and Voltairean in its disrespect for established values. The critic in the *Gazette de France* had concluded: 'It's high time that M. de Stendhal change his style and manner.'

No wonder Beyle could only imagine readers in the distant future (1935 perhaps, or maybe not till a new millennium had dawned) and then just 'the happy few'. The novels, of course, found a large audience well before that date, but in the case of the autobiography his guess was surprisingly accurate. His executor, into whose hands the barely legible manuscript came after Beyle's death, tried rewriting the opening pages in the third person embellished with exactly the kind of artificial diction Beyle abhorred, then gave up. Successive editors, unable to conceive that such a disorderly narrative could be a finished work, presented it as a draft and felt at liberty to eliminate anything that didn't fit current notions of good writing. A full and accurate edition was promised for 1937, but the editor died and the war supervened. So it wasn't till 1949 that French readers saw the full text for the first time, though that edition was still marred by errors in the deciphering of Beyle's difficult handwriting.[8]

To the modern reader the chaotic movement of the opening chapters, far from being a flaw, seems a guarantee of authenticity. The man emerges in all his contradictions – tongue-tied with the women he loved, secretive even with friends, but garrulous and expansive in writing, trusting in the sympathy of the unknown future reader whom he frequently addresses. By allowing the natural flow of memory to direct his pen, and leaving the result uncorrected instead of reordering it chronologically, he achieves the spontaneity and intimacy of conversation, moving back and forth in time, self-questioning, endlessly digressing. The effect may not be uncalculated – he has a comic model in mind that becomes apparent in Chapter XXXIX when the Daru family decide that this feckless young cousin they've taken in should be put to work in the offices of the Ministry of War: 'I am about to be born, as Tristram Shandy says, and the reader will escape these childish stories.'

8. Editor's introduction to *La Vie de Henri Brulard*, Pléiade, II, 1308–1312. As for the diaries, which were never intended for publication, one editor was so shocked by the bad language and 'filthy pornography' of certain passages that he replaced them by dotted lines (while making them available in a supplement).

The title itself with the English Henry instead of Marie-Henri (his godparents' names) has something Shandyesque about it – Brulard is the surname of a great-uncle on his mother's side, prior of a monastery, whom Henri's uncle (teasing his mother about her son's ugliness) said he resembled because the one-year-old infant had an exceptionally large bald head. Self-mocking then, like so many of his pseudonyms (Henry Crocodile and Baron Tenderbum spring to mind), but also, of course, a rejection of the paternal surname[9] and of the scorned and hated father whom, by a strange inversion, he'd started referring to as 'my bastard' after Beyle senior cut off his allowance for five months in the hope of forcing him to choose a career.

But to my ear, 'Brulard' evokes another aspect of Beyle – the hothead ('tête brûlée'), acting on impulse, as when he took off for Italy in September 1811 thinking himself at liberty because Count Daru, who was about to leave on a two-month state visit to Holland with the Emperor, had given him permission to take a few days off. Beyle's absence (spun out to three months) was discovered when Daru sent him an urgent request for the imperial accounts. That and his unauthorised visit to Rome reported by the Direc-

9. He reveals his true surname in Chapter 3, recalling how as a six-year-old he wrote 'Henri Beyle 1789' on all the fresh plaster joins in his grandfather's apartment – an early manifestation of 'egotism'?

tor of Police, Jacques de Norvins (a mean-mouthed, shifty-eyed fellow whose portrait now hangs in the British National Gallery only because it's by Ingres) cost him a promotion and probably explain why he never received the decoration he was entitled to for his service in the Russian campaign.

This escapade must have been one of the follies he had in mind when, in the opening pages, gazing out over Rome, identifying landmarks (including the villa Aldobrandini of Prince Francesco Borghese, whom he'd seen at the battle of Wagram, the day when his friend Monsieur de Noue lost his leg), and congratulating himself that though he's about to reach the sobering age of fifty he hasn't spent his life too badly, he suddenly exclaims: 'But have I ever in the least directed my life?'

That moment – when the urbane persona of Monsieur de Stendhal, former cavalry officer, frequenter of the nobility, author of *Promenades in Rome,* suddenly slips (as though an actor has stripped off the frock coat that proclaims him a gentleman and stands before us in his shirtsleeves and braces) and we hear the voice of plain Henri Beyle is part of what makes this nearly two-hundred-year-old autobiography seem so modern. The admission (half a dozen pages later) of the temptation to embellish – 'How many precautions one must take not to lie! [. . .] No, reader, I wasn't a soldier at Wagram in 1809' – may not disarm all readers but, while no guarantee of absolute honesty, it's an acknowledgement of the twin temptations of autobiography: self-enhancement and self-justification.

The younger Beyle had always tended to inflate the facts and in the case of his military career it stuck. (Almost every online source describes him as a soldier.) The reality was fifteen months in his teens as sub-lieutenant of dragoons (September 1800–December 1801), mainly in garrison among fellow soldiers with whom he had nothing in common,[10] until a recurring fever provided a convenient excuse for sick leave. (His doctor diagnosed his problems as boredom, melancholy and homesickness, common among young recruits.) He resigned his commission during the temporary peace of 1803 and never returned to active service. He found it advantageous, however, to *imply* a military career, attaching the tag 'officier de cavalerie' to the self-ennobling 'Monsieur *de* Stendhal' on the title page of *Rome, Naples et Florence en 1817*, the first work he published under that pseudonym.[11] In the autobiography, he excuses himself for

10. From whose barrack-room talk he reports such gems as the recipe for seduction (or rather, rape) passed on by a Captain Percheron, later Gentleman of the King's Bedchamber under the restored Bourbons [Diary, August 1, 1801].

11. An alternative explanation is that he was then living in Milan, which was once again under Austrian rule after its brief glory as

this vainglory, telling the reader: 'You must understand that forty-five years before your time, it was fashionable to have been a soldier under Napoleon.'

Not just fashionable, but career-advancing. In 1804, living in Paris on a small allowance from his father, he felt the need for gainful employment and asked General Michaud (whom he'd briefly served as unauthorised aide-de-camp) to write him a reference. The good-hearted General said: 'Bring me a draft certificate and I'll sign it.' (Diary, 14 November 1804.) The editor of the diaries, quoting that certificate in full, points out that Beyle had led Michaud to endorse the falsehood that he'd conducted himself bravely at the battle of Castelfranco on January 12, 1801 in which there's no evidence that he'd participated.[12] Indeed the first page of his diary says he didn't leave Milan till February.

Was it a deliberate lie? Immediately after noting Michaud's promise to sign his self-certification, he makes this comment, ostensibly about play-writing:

capital of Napoleon's Kingdom of Italy, so the disguise of a German cavalry officer might get his politically risky book past the Austrian censors. He'd plagiarised some details from Goethe's *Italian Journey* to reinforce this alias. Eventually, however, the Austrians discovered the real identity of this author of 'pernicious books' and banned him from all their Italian domains, refusing his appointment as French consul in Trieste.

12. *Oeuvres intimes*, Pléiade, Vol I, 1198, note 3.

'Before painting a character, lay out his *potential*, that's to say the list of all the acts he could perform.' In other words, he *would* have acted bravely if he'd been at Castelfranco so it was all right to claim it. Let's be kind and call Beyle a fabulist rather than a liar. He was only twenty-one. Who didn't take liberties with the truth at that age? After all he *had* wanted to fight: it wasn't his fault if the action was over.

And to be fair, he *did* participate in most of Napoleon's wars, though only as a war commissioner ('that official despised of soldiers') following the army in the relative comfort of a carriage. It didn't spare him the sight of burnt and pillaged towns or casualties (he was responsible for setting up a military hospital in Vienna). Still, it's telling that when he accompanied the army to Russia in 1812 he took with him twelve notebooks containing the draft of his *History of Painting in Italy* and the manuscript of a play, obviously expecting the leisure to write there. (He lost them in the retreat from Moscow.) The life of an official in French-occupied territories could be very pleasant (dinners, hunting parties, flirtations – not all the locals were hostile), though his duties were sometimes awkward, as when he had to supervise the requisition of precious manuscripts from the Duke of Brunswick's renowned library under the pained eye of its librarian who was at the time teaching him English. Such embarrassments, however, were infinitely preferable to stopping a cannon ball in a cavalry charge.

There's a slightly mean satisfaction in tracking down a falsehood or exaggeration, but there are more rewarding discoveries. Penetrating the disguise of false names and mysterious initials has occupied generations of editors and scholars, and the addictive pleasure of decoding may be a key element in a Beyle obsession. My own began with the mysterious Mme Gherardi in Sebald's *Vertigo*, whom I tracked down in Stendhal's *Rome, Naples et Florence* and *On Love*, where she's a shadowy figure used to voice some Stendhalian notions of love. There had been a real Mme Gherardi back in 1800, a young woman later mentioned in the diary as having 'the most beautiful eyes he'd ever seen' (31 August 1811), but she'd died in childbirth long before the period in which Sebald's story is set. A trivial matter, but I was hooked and it led me to the diaries, where there were still unsolved mysteries, one of which (the identity of the mysterious Mme Lb. referred to on September 27, 1811 in his Florence diary) I managed to decipher, which may earn me a footnote in the next edition, my one chance of immortality.

Beyle has been romanticised as soldier, lover and free spirit by some of his admirers, but his own summation of his life is decidedly unromantic: 'I'm thought to be a wit, a man without feeling, a rake even, but I see that I've been constantly preoccupied with unhappy love affairs' – a judgement he reiterates after two attempts at summarising the significant dates and events of his career: 'The other day meditating on life in the lonely path above Lake Albano I realised that my life could be summed up by the following names, of which I wrote the initials in the dust with my cane.' They are, of course, the names of the dozen women he loved, only six of whom he actually 'had' (but couldn't keep). Reflecting on their role in his life, he concludes: 'I have never really been ambitious, though I believed myself ambitious in 1811. The habitual state of my life has been that of a man unhappy in love.'

There'd been no lack of sex in his life, of course – inn servants or girls on the street (for which he paid the inevitable penalty) and then for several years a young opera-singer mistress, the devoted 'little Angel', whose meagre salary at the Opéra comique he supplemented with 'gifts'.[13] He seems to have been good at giving his partners pleasure if the following (in his Franglais) isn't a boast: 'I make that one or two every day, she [Angeline] five, six and sometimes neuf fois.' (Diary, 17 March 1811.) But the great love he dreamed of mostly eluded him (or proved delusory as in the case of Angela Pietragrua).

13. Angeline Bereyter, who, among other roles, performed Cherubino in the 1807 Paris premiere of *Le Nozze di Figaro*.

A woman who offers a key to that unhappiness and occupies the most space in the diaries (from 1809 to 1811) is Count Daru's young wife, Alexandrine (always concealed by pseudonyms, sometimes several on the same page to really muddy the waters). Conventional editors found it puzzling that a young man should be so obsessed with the mother of a growing family. But you don't need to be a Freudian to see that's part of the attraction. Not only was Alexandrine Daru the same physical type as his mother [14] but when Beyle first got to know her on his return from Brunswick early in 1809 she was twenty-six with two little girls, a small boy and a babe in arms – a similar configuration to the family of his childhood, with the extra baby that would have been his third sibling if mother and infant hadn't died of a botched delivery when he was seven. By the time they met again in Vienna at the end of 1809 he was clearly in the first throes of love. During the month she spent there, his diary recounts his supremely awkward attempts to court her, summed up by the ironic heading in his peculiar English that he added later: 'The life and sentiments of silencious Harry'.

14. No portrait of his mother exists, but he describes her as plump (unsurprisingly, given the four pregnancies that followed his own birth), dark-haired, rosy-cheeked, brown-eyed. One can guess what she looked like by the portraits of Beyle's sisters, Pauline and Zénaïde (easily located online, as is a portrait of Alexandrine Daru).

Among the Viennese sights he escorted her to was the anatomy museum, where (he recalls later[15]) she was particularly interested in the obstetrics display where a demonstrator manipulated the wax models of the birth process and its hazards. There's a tragic irony here in that the spectators were a young man whose mother had died in childbirth and a woman who'd meet the same fate six years later (in 1815, after bearing her eighth child). No wonder that in the famous 'fiasco' at the brothel with his friends in 1821 he was unable to perform with the beautiful young woman presented for their pleasure whose name, fatefully, was Alexandrine.[16] In *Souvenirs d' Egotisme*, he attributed his failure to thoughts of Metilde, another dead love. Discretion prohibited any link to Alexandrine Daru, but the connection is there for a modern reader.

However daringly Beyle had plotted his courtship of Mme Daru (alternating between the language of a military campaign and that of an 18th-century novel), he clearly behaved with all the awkwardness of a boy with a crush, as he recognises on Monte Albano when he says, after naming the four women for whom he'd

15. Diary, 27 September 1811 (*Oeuvres intimes*, Pléiade I, 785).
16. She was seventeen or eighteen, he thought, with the beauty of a Titian, and new to the trade. Six months later she was being maintained by some rich Englishmen and he would see her pass in a fine carriage, but before long she'd coarsened like her fellow-workers.

felt the greatest passion: 'With all the former and with several others I was always a child and thus I had little success.'

It's not just coincidence, surely, that three of the women he loved (Angela Pietragrua, Alexandrine Daru and Metilde Dembowski) had young sons; watching them together, he must have felt all he'd been deprived of by his mother's death. That a child's feelings for a parent (especially one lost young) may affect relationships in adult life is no surprise, though whether Beyle saw the connection isn't clear. He certainly recognised his childhood passion for his mother and jealousy of his father (anticipating Freud by half a century): 'I wanted to cover her with kisses and that there should be no clothing . . . I detested my father when he interrupted our kisses.' No doubt it's because he lost his mother so young without going through the gradual detachment and adolescent ambivalence that suppress the early bond that he recalls it so vividly. There'd been no mother-substitute in his childhood apart from the servant Marion. His mother's younger sister, Séraphie, a devout and narrow-minded woman, took over the care of the children until her own death from unspecified illness six years later, but she clearly found it hard to manage this difficult small boy and there was nothing but mutual dislike between them. Of course, he had his allies in the kitchen (especially the young man-servant Lambert, whose death he wept over as bitterly as his mother's), and he found a 'true' father and better teacher in his grandfather, but it wasn't the same. It was only when he was sent to stay with his newly-married uncle the summer following his mother's death that, all too briefly, he found the maternal tenderness and understanding he needed with his new young aunt and her sisters – a patch of sunlight in the gloomy narrative of his childhood.

The movement of the autobiography is from happiness lost – 'all the joy of childhood ended with my mother's death' – to happiness recovered when he arrives in Milan and meets (though he doesn't name her) Angela Pietragrua. His memories are so overwhelming at that point that the writing simply collapses into incoherence and he abandons the manuscript unfinished.[17]

A continuation already existed, however, in the lifelong diary he'd started in Milan two days after his eighteenth birthday. The first entry, dated in the Revolutionary style *28th Germinal year IX* [April 18, 1801], begins: 'I am going to write the history of my life day by day. I don't know if I shall have the strength to fulfil this project, already begun in Paris. There's an incorrect expression already; there'll be

17. Possibly because though he says it would spoil such happiness to describe it, his love for Angela Pietragrua is now sullied by his later knowledge of her venality.

28

a lot because I've decided not to bother about them and never to erase.' The autobiographical impulse, along with the refusal of conventional style, began early.

That diary, maintained faithfully for the next sixteen years (and thereafter reconstituted by his editors from innumerable notes on scraps of paper or marginalia in books) gives a detailed insight into his development, both personal and intellectual. You watch him grow from the inarticulate boy to a self-assured man, guided by the classical maxim '*Nosce te ipsum*' – 'Know thyself' – that at twenty-eight he'd seen as the principal aim of his diary (August 10, 1811).

It's a fascinating life-record though the endless self-analysis can become tedious. Young Beyle is pretentious, convinced of his intellectual superiority, hard even cruel in his judgements of others, especially his rivals in the competitive world of the Napoleonic administration. Self-absorbed certainly, yet disarmingly honest about himself at times – your judgement of him wavers from page to page. But there's no denying his clear-sightedness about some of the experiences he lived through, which makes it a document of the times as well as the history of a private life. In December 1804 (not yet twenty-two), after watching the Pope and the Emperor arrive at Notre Dame for the coronation, he described it as an 'alliance of charlatans [. . .] religion consecrating tyranny in the name of the happiness of mankind'. Eventually, he recognised the Emperor as a force for modernisation and reform, though when Napoleon returned from Elba he didn't rush to his side, unlike his cousin, the ever-loyal Count Daru. Nonetheless, on July 25, 1815 (a month after Waterloo) he drew a candle-snuffer in his diary to symbolise the extinction of the enlightened policies of the Empire.

The diary has one important advantage: it was private, so could be more intimately revealing than the autobiography which he hoped would be published. But the ongoing record of a life isn't the same as the retrospective account. Most importantly, it lacks the childhood, so often the crucial element of a life history. In Beyle's case, particularly, we need the story of his relationship with his mother and his reaction to her death to make sense of all those unhappy love affairs that, to the man looking back in his fifties, seemed to define his life more than his experiences in the Empire or his peripatetic existence after its collapse.

But does the autobiography, as at least one unsympathetic reader has judged, exaggerate that childhood misery? Somerset Maugham in his introduction to *The Red and the Black* remarked:

Like all children, he [Henri Beyle] looked upon ordinary restraints as the exercise of outrageous tyranny;

and when . . . he was not allowed to do exactly as he chose, regarded himself as treated with monstrous cruelty. In this he resembled most children, but most children, when they grow up, forget their grievances. Stendhal was unusual in that, at fifty-three, he harboured his old resentments.[18]

One might have expected more sympathy from Maugham, who lost his own beloved mother at eight and was sent to live with an austere, elderly vicar-uncle and aunt, then to boarding-school where he was mocked for his stammer. Instead, he treats Beyle with the 'no nonsense' attitude of the emotionally repressed. The boy, he says, far from being ill-treated, simply received the typical education of his class. To this reader at least, the tutor Father Raillane, who kept an unhygienic cage of canaries next to his young charge's bed, sounds unsuitable even by the standards of the time, quite apart from his teaching Ptolemaic astronomy 'because it was approved by the church'.[19]

As for Beyle's complaint that he'd had no playmates of his own age, Maugham dismisses it, citing his little

18. *Ten Novels and Their Authors*, 1954.
19. Another Beyliste myth is that Beyle was educated by a Jesuit, simply because he uses that term for Raillane. But the Jesuits had been expelled from France in 1764 and suppressed by the Pope in 1773. In common parlance 'Jesuit' had come to mean 'a devious or hypocritical person' and was one of the anti-clerical Beyle's favourite terms of abuse.

sisters and the two boys who shared his lessons. But what young Henri longed for was the freedom to roam with the boys whom he saw from a distance playing marbles or bathing in the river. A sedate walk with his tutor or a carriage ride with an elderly aunt were no substitute for the rough-and-tumble adventures of boyhood. In many ways his upbringing made him distrust others until he encountered the few fellow-spirits who would become friends.

Fortunately, our understanding of child psychology and in particular of a child's response to bereavement has expanded since Maugham's time. And I'm on Beyle's side here.[20] I feel for that unhappy child whose emotional development was warped and who consequently never quite found what he wanted in life. According to Victor Brombert, that would make me a 'Brulardist', part of 'the extreme wing of the Beylist sect'. I don't care. I'm drawn to Henri Beyle, not just because I too lost a parent in childhood, but because complicated individuals have always interested me more than sunny, positive, well-adjusted types. Perhaps (though my own childhood was mainly happy) I was primed by all those Victorian classics I read to

20. As the big sister of a 'difficult' small brother, I fantasise that an older sister might have defended young Henri against uncomprehending adults and helped him avoid trouble. Big sisters are often bossy – I know I was – but they can be allies, and my brother told me years later that 'we'd made a good team against the grown-ups'.

identify with the survivors of unhappy childhoods.

Still, I recognise there's much that Beyle doesn't make allowance for in the family situation. The tutor Raillane arrived in December 1792; a month later the king was guillotined (two days before Henri's tenth birthday) and by September that year the Reign of Terror had begun. Beyle maintains it was 'mild' in Grenoble but nonetheless his father was on the list of suspects. What actually ensued is unclear. The editor of the personal writings, Victor Del Litto, says that Cherubin Beyle was imprisoned for eleven and a half months,[21] but Beyle claims that Seraphie's efforts obtained delays and that in fact his father was spending the nights with them in the grandfather's house. However, he does admit that he only claims to be right in what concerns his own feelings and that he's always had a poor memory for facts. Whatever the case, it was indisputably a time of great anxiety in the family, which may explain some of the isolation that the boy experienced as harsh. The 'tyranny' of Father Raillane soon came to an end as the priest appears to have been deported to French Guiana in accordance with the decree that all priests who'd refused to take the oath of loyalty to the Constitution must leave the country.[22] After a brief interlude with a nicer but even less competent tutor, young Beyle entered the

21. Pléiade, vol. 2, 1397, note 8.
22. Pléiade, vol 2, 1391, note 1.

newly established Ecole Centrale where at last he had decent teachers and (after getting his 'inordinate pride' knocked out of him in the playground) a few friends.

I visited Grenoble a few years ago, hoping to see the Stendhal manuscripts which are kept at the municipal library. My earlier experience in French archives, when you were simply handed a file box and could read through a bundle of 200-year-old letters, had led me to expect easy access, but the days of being allowed to handle such fragile pieces of the past are over. By good luck, however, my visit coincided with European Heritage weekend and I joined a group admitted to the darkened room to see the manuscript of the autobiography. It was open at a page with a sketch map of the floorplan of the family apartment, empty for several years after his mother's death during which the children lived in their grandfather's house, though later Henri would sneak back to escape family life. Recalling his eleven-year-old self, alone in the empty salon trying to write a comedy, he drew a tiny stick-figure marked H for Henri. It was strangely moving to see it.

But one of the events I attended in Grenoble had a hero-worshipping tone that made me wish for an acerbic interruption from Beyle's ghost. The literary theorist Gerard Genette finds such 'fetichization' of the author delusionary:

> [I]n his novels and in his correspondence, in his essays and in his memoirs, Beyle is always present but almost always masked or in disguise, and it is not without significance that his most directly 'autobiographical' work has as its title a name that is neither that of the author, nor that of its hero: Stendhal covers Henri Brulard, who covers Henri Beyle – who in turn imperceptibly displaces the Henri Beyle of legal status, who is not at all to be confused with the other three, and forever eludes us.[23]

Genette wrote this at a moment when the 'Death of the Author' had become part of the credo of literary theorists, though he's certainly right in drawing attention to the slippery nature of the 'author' in question here. The Beyle we think we know, he concludes, is 'only one of Stendhal's characters'. But do we have to accept that judgement? There were, after all, years of diaries (1800–1817) before Beyle published anything under the name Stendhal (and even longer before he became publicly identified by the name). The fact that the diaries were eventually published as Stendhal's doesn't make them any less

23. Gerard Genette, 'Stendhal', *Figures* 2, 1968, transl. Alan Sheridan, p. 149.

Beyle's. Of course, the 'self' in a diary is a projection that may solidify in both the diarist's and his readers' minds into a 'character', but it seems unduly dogmatic to conflate the young diarist with his much later persona.

Very few authors, however, attract the kind of cult that a cerebral theorist like Genette deplored. And now that the internet perpetuates some of the half-truths and myths around Stendhal,[24] it's harder than ever to distinguish between the individual and his persona. Perhaps it's right to acknowledge that we all have our own Beyle, the product of an inevitably selective reading shaped by our own biases and predilections. I've focused here on Beyle the untrustworthy self-recorder, whose reputation needs demystifying. But I might just as easily have written about Beyle the reader – that seventeen-year-old following the army through the Alps already had a portmanteau containing fifty-eight books, and the diaries record his self-education in psychology and political theory as well as several literatures. An autodidact with a poor memory (or so he said), he only retained

24. An example is the so-called 'Stendhal syndrome', based on a naive and partial reading of an episode in one of his travel books that has a very different and politically subversive message if you read the whole of it. The irony there is that a characteristically Stendhalian pose intended to distract the Austrian censors has taken in a modern psychiatrist.

what fitted his own views (like many of us), but it infused the later novels with the sharp critical perspective that contributed to their uniqueness.

I t's time I confessed that 'my' Beyle now exists in a novel set in 1811. It's not the most attractive period of his life. As he acknowledges in the autobiography, he was a conceited young fop with his dandy's wardrobe – forty-two shirts (twenty-seven with ruffles) and eighteen waistcoats (Diary, 29 June 1810) – and his coachman waiting for him outside the fashionable café Hardy with one of his two carriages. It's the period of his high life – two hours at the office most days, five or six twice a week, social calls, the café, a play or opera every night, and a late supper with his little Angel in the charming apartment he shared with a friend – but the play he was writing, or the great works he planned, endlessly postponed for lack of time.

I would never have given so much time to this young buck if it hadn't been for an unexpected detail in his diary. In September 1811 on that ill-judged, career-wrecking trip to Italy, he mentions finding a book by Mary Wollstonecraft in the Paris–Milan stagecoach. I was as surprised as he was by its presence in the depths of the French countryside and it made me bring into being its reader, an imagined woman traveller with whom Beyle has to share the narrative focus. But it also led me to explore how Beyle the would-be lady-killer (in full martial array as he transfers his infatuation with Mme Daru to the more easily conquerable Angela Pietragrua) could develop into the man who fifteen years later would make this unexpected declaration:

> The admission of women to complete equality would be the surest mark of civilisation; it would double the intellectual capacity of the human race and its potential for happiness.[25]

It's astonishing for its time, not least in its emphasis on women's intellectual potential. Although there'd been a feminist element in the early stages of the Revolution, Napoleon's Civil Code put an end to such aspirations and the Restoration only reinforced conservative views. But in some ways Beyle was always ahead of his times and already a few passages in the 1811 diary suggest an awareness of how social conventions and an ill-conceived feminine education restricted women's development. While he'd skimmed only a few pages of the Wollstonecraft book in the diligence (her last unfinished novel, set in a madhouse), I saw how its unknown reader might play a tiny role in the evolution of his view of women.

25. *Rome, Naples et Florence*, 1826.

Of course, I had huge misgivings about the liberties I was taking, though I invented only in the few but convenient gaps in his diary. I wasn't alone, however: several other novels (both French and English) use Henri Beyle or Monsieur de Stendhal as a character. In that sense Genette was right. Beyle/Stendhal, whichever we want to call him, *has* become a fiction. But he's not alone in that respect. With the rise of the biographical novel, one of the currently most attractive subjects for writers appears to be the life of another writer. Tolstoy, Henry James, Thomas Mann, Virginia Woolf, Dorothy Richardson, to name a few, have all received fictional treatment – Beyle is in good company.

Would he have minded the way in which I and others have exploited his story? He might have laughed at the incongruity of it, winced at the revelation of certain secrets or shaken his head over misreadings, but longing for recognition as he did, I suspect he'd have welcomed any chance of staying alive and tipped his hat to his portrayers. My hope is that anyone who meets 'my' Beyle will head straight to the man's own inimitable autobiographical writings to meet the original.

CHARLES BOYLE ❧ In the Provinces

I n August 2016 I took a photograph of Henri
Beyle, aka Stendhal, in Notting Hill. He was
crossing the road, over to the side of the Gate
Cinema. I recognised him because he was wearing
an oversized overcoat and green sunglasses, the same
outfit he wore when he followed a woman he loved to
Volterra in Tuscany in 1819. In 2016, despite a flower-
patterned shopping bag slung over his shoulder, he
looked like a brigand. I wanted to go after him but he
was walking fast and luckily for both of us the lights
changed. Beyle in *Memoirs of an Egotist* remarks that
after he had started to publish he was 'quite often'
approached by people who wanted to congratulate
him: 'The compliment and my reply done with, we
didn't know what to say to each other.' When Beyle
met Byron in Milan in 1816, 'I tried to speak, and
uttered only commonplaces, which were of no help
against the silence which this evening prevailed
amongst the circle.'

In 1819 the overcoat and the sunglasses were worn
as a disguise. Metilde Dembowski had travelled from
Milan to Volterra to see her sons at their school and

she had forbidden Beyle to follow her. But she too recognised him as soon as she saw him. She sent him packing. Beyle attempted to turn this episode into fiction, renaming himself and Metilde and introducing a lesbian duchess, but he stalled after the first chapter. How to proceed? Maybe just leave it there. This was the premise of my own short novel about Beyle, *An Overcoat: Scenes from the Afterlife of H.B.* (2017): rejected but unable to stop loving – can't stay, can't leave – he is stranded for ever in a provincial small town.

According to Doris Lessing (in her introduction to Andrew Brown's translation of Beyle's *Memoirs of an Egotist*, published in 2003), 'The ideal lover of Stendhal comes, as he did, from a family of conventional people in a provincial town . . .' I put my hand up. I think Lessing meant that if you have dullness to rebel against, and are hungry for something more in life, then Stendhal is your guy. I take my hand down. Beyle was born in the provincial town of Grenoble and couldn't wait to leave. I was born in a dormitory suburb of Leeds and was happy to wait to leave for as long as it took and I have always felt provincial (and/ or provisional). This is stupid: although there is a sense in which *all* childhoods are provincial, lived in the shadow of grown-ups whether in Mayfair or in a dormitory suburb, I am white and male and was born into the middle class of one of the richest countries in the world. I am steeped in privilege. My feeling provincial is an evasion of sorts; but it *is* what I feel.

The provinces take up most space on the maps. Most people live there. Most of the derogatory connotations of the word 'provincial' – small-mindedness, bigotry and the like – derive from the snobbishness and insecurity of those who are afraid to be themselves thought mediocre. Among them, people who won the lottery at birth and who know they have done nothing to deserve it. There was a period in the 1950s and the early 1960s – after my father died and I was sent to a prep school – when I *embraced* mediocrity. In my end-of-term exams I came nearer the bottom of the class than the top and that never worried me. A teacher's comment in a school report in May 1963 nailed me: 'No flair but he plods on.' Flair was show-biz and flashy. To have flair was to put your head above the parapet, where you were liable to get shot.

My handwritten list of books read in 1963 at that boarding school includes the usual suspects, Rider Haggard and Conan Doyle and John Buchan and C. S. Forester, plus Alistair MacLean and Hammond Innes; just two women writers and one translation in the list of forty titles. (That school closed in 2014, following sex abuse scandals.) But then a few years later, at an all-boys public school in Scotland, I found a way through: Lawrence and Blake, William Faulkner and Malcolm Lowry, David Storey and Alan Sillitoe. Still no women; but also no Waugh and no Wodehouse, and a bias towards writers who themselves have been described as provincial. (In 2023 the Scottish Child Abuse Inquiry published a report on that school detailing evidence of violence, bullying and sex abuse from the 1950s through to 2014.) I was a conformist boy at a bad school who ran when he was told to run, walked when he was told to walk. Reading was going undercover.

I mean that both figuratively and literally: reading with a torch under the bedclothes after lights-out, daring someone, anyone, to stop me. Without the thrill of transgression books are a poor sport. Beyle, in *The Life of Henry Brulard*, steals books by Voltaire from an edition of forty in his father's glass-fronted bookcase, often locked: 'I took down two and spread the rest out a little, it didn't show.' I know that trick. Shoplifters know it too. I was taught how to shoplift in around 1971 by a teenager at a school for bad boys in Northamptonshire; his name was O'Boyle, no more different from my own name than that of the man I am writing about here – or that of Henry Bell, another man I met in my twenties at a time when I was ripe for being led astray, if only by a letter or two

– and he was reading Dostoevsky and he took me into a department store in town on a Saturday afternoon and asked me what I wanted. A leather jacket? I must have wanted something but I had no idea what; I already had so much, whether I wanted it or not.

Back to Beyle – stealing from his grandfather this time: waiting, waiting, until his grandfather leaves the room and then 'Presto, I went into the study at L, and stole a book.' It barely matters *which* book. He made a habit of this. 'I wouldn't be able to express the excitement with which I read those books.'

I know that I read Faulkner's *As I Lay Dying* at the age of sixteen because there is my pencilled name and a date, March 1967, on the flyleaf of my copy of that book which I lent to a friend and which he returned to me forty-nine years later, in 2016, in a wine bar in London near Victoria station, passing through. He still hadn't got round to reading it; or if he had, he couldn't remember it. My own memory of the book is hazy but what I have always remembered is that, as it says on the back cover, it was written 'in six summer weeks during night-shifts at the local power station'.

My reading choices were influenced by a Protestant work ethic embedded at home, at school and in English middle-class life more generally. Save money, spend it wisely. Save it for a *rainy day*. The overriding message was that pleasure had to be earned; the under-riding message was that the only pleasure on offer was that of working for it. How this translated into books was roughly as follows: reading is play-time, a leisure activity conducted in the off-hours, not work – no one is *paying* me to read – and nor is the production of reading matter work, in the way that making cast-iron drainpipes (my father's job) is work, so writing too is best conducted in the off-hours (or during night-shifts at a power station). In this nation of shopkeepers there is a pleasing symmetry here: the books are balanced. Obviously, people with inherited income have a lot of off-hours, and I can't stop them using that time to write books, but this is cheating because off-hours have to be earned, by work.

Although later in life I chose not to renew my subscription to that ethic, it was formative. I still cannot see writing as a *job*. I underlined passages in *Biographia Literaria* – the date on the flyleaf of my copy: November 1969 – in which Coleridge insists on the importance for writers of being 'something besides an author', of not being 'a mere literary man', of not relying on writing for an income (*'never pursue literature as a trade'*, his italics), of having 'habits of active life and daily intercourse with the stir of the world'. That T. S. Eliot and Wallace Stevens had jobs in offices and that William Carlos Williams and

Chekhov were practising doctors were marks in their favour.

My reading choices were also influenced by the only thing that school in Scotland taught me, a distrust of institutions. My attachment to Beyle – as to every other writer who has meant much to me – was enabled by no one *telling* me to read him. This is why, despite studying Eng Lit at Cambridge, I didn't get round to reading *Middlemarch* and *Vanity Fair* until I was in my sixties: I was too busy avoiding the official reading list by reading *other* books. I had everything handed to me on a plate and I chose to worry about the plate.

And this is why, when I want to re-acquaint myself with Beyle, I'll often go not to the capital cities but to the hinterland, the provinces, the travel books he wrote for quick money: bad hotels, bedbugs, cold coffee, rain and mud and streets smelling of cabbage and the luggage left in coaches, never recovered, and occasionally something marvellous: 'As I came out, I met a peasant woman carrying a peacock in a basket on her head.'

I read *The Red and the Black* in the late 1960s but Beyle did not enter my bloodstream until the early 1990s, when I stumbled across a second-hand copy of *Memoirs of an Egotist* (in the translation by David

Ellis published by D. J. Enright at Chatto & Windus in 1975). This is a short, haphazard, improvisatory memoir of his life in Paris, and a trip to London, in the 1820s; Beyle started writing it on 20 June 1832 and abandoned it – mid-chapter, mid-paragraph: 'It's become too hot to think' – two weeks later. It is a record of 'daily intercourse with the stir of the world'.

The author was named on the title page as Stendhal but this wasn't the author of the novel I had read in my teens. This was – as he names himself in the book in cod Italian on the tombstone he designs for himself, 'a marble plaque in the form of a playing card' – 'Errico Beyle'. I was intrigued rather than puzzled; I had learned by then that authors are often not who you think they are. Listening to an author in person has sometimes switched me on to work that had previously left me cold, and sometimes turned me off from work I had previously liked. In this case, Beyle sent me back to the novels for enriched re-readings.

A pedestrian feature of *Egotist* is Beyle's spelling-out of the incomes of the people he writes about. M. de Lussinge had 'an income of 22,000 or 23,000 francs'; 'His meanness always made him dress badly and he took advantage of our strolls together to work out reckonings of personal expense for a bachelor living alone in Paris.' M. Barot – 'good-looking and without any liveliness of mind whatsoever' – had 'an income of 80,000 francs a year'. M. Poitevin 'had a pension of 1,200 francs and a post worth 1,500 francs', and 'On that he was one of the best-dressed young men in Paris'. M. de Tracy 'was born about 1765 with an income of 300,000 francs'. M. de Barral had a father ('a gentleman through and through'; Beyle's father left him nothing but debts) who 'allocated him 6,000 francs a year'. At the time Beyle is writing, de Barral 'has become rich; he has at least 20,000 francs a year, and with all this money he's become atrociously mean'.

Of course Beyle was interested in money: he had arrived in Paris as a scholarship boy from the provinces with ambitions beyond his means. Money is there in the novels too. The opening paragraphs of *The Red and the Black* introduce the picture-postcard town of Verrières: white houses with red-tiled roofs, a river flowing beneath ruined battlements, idyllic except for the noise of 'massive hammers falling with a boom that makes the street tremble'. The noise comes from a factory owned by the mayor, M. de Rênal, who prunes his trees to provide shade because that's all a tree is good for when, 'unlike the useful walnut, it doesn't bring in any money'. Beyle adds: 'Here is the mighty phrase that determines everything at Verrières: BRING IN MONEY. All by itself it represents the habitual thinking of more than three-quarters of the inhabitants.' M. de Rênal offers Julien Sorel, the son of a sawyer, who has learned

Latin and is therefore almost a priest, 300 francs a year plus meals to tutor his children; Julien's father negotiates the deal up to 400 francs a year, to be paid monthly in advance, plus a clothing allowance. And so, with a calculated mention of M. de Rênal's much younger wife, who has 'a certain air of naturalness and youth in her walk', the novel begins.

As a sixteen-year-old boy at an all-boys boarding school I didn't know much about anything, and even less about girls. Sex was a state secret wrapped in whispers and rumour. This was one reason, maybe the main one, why I was going undercover: to find out. Beyle in his early teens, leafing through 'the quarto volumes of Pliny' in his grandfather's study: 'I was looking especially for the natural history of *woman*.' Ben Sonnenberg in his memoir *Lost Property*: 'For me, as doubtless for many men, a love of literature began in masturbation and was always linked to pornography.'

Male novelists of the 19th century who fucked servant girls while writing about love are not much help here. (Though a combination of exalted feeling and worldly cynicism seems to be what many readers require of literature.) Julien Sorel achieves social success by expressing, eloquently, the opposite of what he believes ('he ended up boring himself with the sound of his own voice'), and conducts his love life with similar feints and bluffs: 'If she sees how much I adore her, I shall lose her.' Beyle in *The Red and the Black* was seeking to portray a society in which youthful talent can only succeed by hypocrisy, but I didn't have that angle at the time I first read it (I'm too impatient to read the editor's or translator's introductions) and I took the emphasis on deceit, and the pursuit of women by men as a form of military campaign, as gospel. I wasn't wholly wrong; most satire is half in love with what is being satirised. Giulio in *The Abbess of Castro*, determined to visit the woman he loves, who has been locked away by her father in a convent, seeks advice 'as to how best to manage this amorous and military affair': travel in disguise, he is told; tell lies (and if 'you cannot find any useful lie to tell, then speak lies at random'); do not approach the town directly, and 'enter from the side opposite to that you're coming from'. In *Memoirs of an Egotist* Beyle recalls the town of Volterra as 'the scene of one of my most daring exploits in my war against Metilde'.

Metilde rejected Beyle. Probably she just didn't fancy him (he was short and stout and wore a toupee). Of the twelve women whose initials he scratched in the sand on a path above Lake Albano in 1835 – a *V*, six *A*s, three *M*s, a *C* and a *G*: the women who had been his 'passionate preoccupation' – more than half he hadn't slept with, and not because he didn't want to. He claimed to have spent much of his life falling in love and off horses – and in his novels the latter is often a consequence of the former. In *Lucien Leuwen* Mme de Chasteller knows that she is loved by Lucien when she sees him 'falling off his horse twice under my window'. In *The Red and the Black*, hearing that Julien has tumbled off his horse into the mud of the rue du Bac, the woman he loves 'tried in vain to stifle a peal of laughter'. It's worth noting that like a number of authors whose fans tend to be rather solemn – Beckett, Kafka, Bernhard – Beyle was a *comic* writer.

I don't know how you'd measure this but I'd wager that literature has messed up more relationships than it hasn't. Writers and readers can be dangerous characters. The writer in Noah Baumbach's film *The Squid and the Whale* is a monster in a corduroy jacket (I mean the one with a beard; his wife writes too but this can be ignored until she starts to get published, when it becomes a problem); his priggish son attempts to charm a girl by telling her what a great writer Kafka was ('Kafka-esque', even). In Walker Percy's *The Moviegoer*, the reader of *The Charterhouse of Parma* encountered by the narrator on a day-long bus journey is a menace to himself and all women. 'He is a romantic. His posture is the first clue: it is too good to be true, this distillation of all graceful slumps.' He will 'scare the wits out of some girl with his great choking silences, want her so desperately that by his own peculiar logic he can't have her; or, having her, jump another ten miles beyond both of them and end by fleeing to the islands where, propped at the rail of his ship in some rancid port, he will ponder his own loneliness.'

A reader and a writer for decades, I sometimes feel ambivalent about the whole enterprise. It hasn't got us to a good place. Not its job, I know. And then I am ambivalent about my ambivalence: is this honesty or evasion? Am I as see-through as the reader on the bus? The first paragraph of Roland Barthes' essay 'The Death of the Author' – published in 1967, that year again – ends thus: 'Writing is that neutral, composite, oblique space where our subject slips away, the negative where all identity is lost, starting with the very identity of the body writing.' There speaks an intellectual Frenchman. Beyle, in contrast, feels oddly English; but he dedicated much of his life to slipping away.

He had several hundred pen names. He disavowed authorship: in the preface to his first novel, *Armance*, he claims to be only the editor, the true author being 'a woman of character' who 'has asked my unworthy self to correct the style'. He plagiarised without shame, or even worry. He was always getting on coaches, moving from one rented room to another, from one love affair to another. Not a keeper. In his non-fiction, unreliable narration was his default mode. He starts writing *A Roman Journal* at a table from which 'I can see three-fourths of Rome; and across from me, at the other end of town, the cupola of St Peter's rises majestically.' No: he was writing in a room at the Hôtel de Valois, 71 rue de Richelieu, Paris. He starts writing *The Life of Henry Brulard* on 16 October 1832, 'on the Janiculum Hill in Rome', where he recalls being present at the battle of Wagram in 1809, where 'my friend, M. de Noue, had his leg taken off'. Again, no: he was writing in 1835, and not in Rome, and on the date of the battle he was lying ill in Vienna – 'stretched out on a chaise longue, with a splitting headache and the fidgets', he wrote to his sister. He was very fond of his sister.

What – or who – was Beyle continually slipping away *from*? The bailiffs, sometimes, but not his readers. The candour of his writing is disarming. In *Brulard* Beyle he can remember his grandfather's powdered wig – 'it had three rows of curls' – but not when he died: 'Was it in 1807 or 1813? I have no rec-ollection.' Recalling his failures in love he suddenly remembers a woman in Paris 'around 1829': 'she had on a dress of black velvet that day – near the Rue du Helder or the Rue du Mont-Blanc'. Precision allied to imprecision, a muddying of the water, is a means of seducing the reader into trusting him – because who can *not* trust someone who openly admits they may have got some of the circumstantial details wrong? He knows that the most convincing story is the one with holes in it. (Roberto Bolaño uses this rhetorical device often: 'I've forgotten the name of the street; sometimes I think it was called the Aurora, but maybe I'm getting mixed up.')

About evasions, also this: if, as someone from the wrong side of the tracks, you perceive that your route to self-fulfilment is blocked by a conspiracy of dunces – the honourable members of a club whose rules are designed to protect their status – then you may well be tempted yourself to adopt the ploys of conspiracy: codes, bluffs, concealment, secrecy, disguise . . . Which happen to be the stuff of many plots in fiction, Beyle's not least. And also the stuff of card games. And strategies that young children take to with glee, seizing a little agency in a world ruled by adults.

Not a few of Beyle's evasions and ambivalences mirror my own, such a tangle and confusion that it occurred to me one day – while walking down the Uxbridge Road, or was it while swimming lengths in the pool in Acton? – that perhaps fiction rather than literary criticism was the way to look into this.

Carelessness, or apparent carelessness, with dates and times and latitudes and longitudes is a Beyle trademark. Robert Adams's *Stendhal* has an appendix listing 'some of the major slips, inconsistencies, oversights, and verbal faults in Stendhal's two major novels' (these include a character who is married and then, conveniently, not). Beyle would have shrugged. Fussing about detail was bourgeois. To be perceived as an *amateur* was important to him. When he shut himself up in a fourth-floor room on the rue Caumartin in 1838 to write *The Charterhouse of Parma* – which he did, famously, in 53 days – the concierge was instructed to tell visitors that he had gone hunting and was out of town, not that he shouldn't be interrupted because he was *working*. He disdained nit-picking, careerism, sentimentality, florid prose, factories, the English ('The logic of the English . . . becomes confused and at a loss as soon as slightly abstract subjects are involved') and the northern, chilly, Protestant work ethic.

Or did he? He was a self-made man, which involves a huge amount of *making*: much more than allowing others, or the 'system', to do it for you. The freelance life is not glamorous: chasing money, chasing openings that suddenly close, knowing when to speak and when to curb one's tongue, all these involve far more effort and perseverance (and sheer luck) than taking a steady job to pay off the mortgage. Beyle often had to pick himself up and start again, notably after the abdication of Napoleon in 1814 and the restoration of the Bourbon monarchy, when he lost his salary and his fine apartment and was deeply in debt and had to jostle for employment under a regime he reckoned 'like fetid slime'. Doing this while at the same time affecting to despise 9-to-5 drudgery is a doubling-down on work.

B eyle's inability to *sit still* was confusing to others. Berlioz: 'Who is this rotund little man with the malicious smile, who wants to appear serious?' Upstart? Cad? Is he amusing, or is he making fun of *us*? Something fox-like here. I think Berlioz caught him on an off-day: more often Beyle affected wit rather than seriousness, the latter carrying the risk that he might appear too earnest.

He *was* serious, not least about his writing. When *The Charterhouse* received an admiring 60-page review from Balzac he was head-over-heels: 'You have taken pity on an orphan abandoned in the street.' He didn't expect his memoir books to be published in his lifetime but he did expect them to be published at some time – ten, twenty, a hundred years after his death – and teased his future editors with bad handwriting and coded, inconsistent abbreviations. And he was serious too about his quest for 'happiness', for which honesty and self-knowledge were the first steps – no pressure, then. But everything with Beyle took a roundabout route. He relished good food and wine, good clothes (the shirts, the waistcoats), opera, books, travel, high-table talk about ideas, and he wanted to be made a baron and a member of the Académie Française, and though none of these is inimical to happiness, may even be a means to that end, to be in a position to enjoy them he had to play by the club rules. He was good at self-sabotage, a trait he shared with the protagonists in his fiction: Julien Sorel 'made tremendous efforts to destroy what was most lovable in himself'. He was serious about love, too; but, acutely aware of his diffidence and that he was short and stout, his knowledge that he was most attractive to women when he was most 'natural' compelled him to strive to *appear* natural, with predictably bad results.

Performance, the *wanting to appear*, was always going to be a problem. After you have taken one pen name, told one lie – and who doesn't at times feel the need for an undercover life? A double life? – the gates are open: you tell a second lie to cover the first, and if one pen name why not another and another? Does this matter? Yes, even though you are always going to be misunderstood. In 1809, riding over the bodies of dead soldiers in Ebersberg in Bavaria in a carriage whose wheels squelched out their entrails,

Beyle wanted to vomit, and so 'I began talking in order to take my mind off this frightful sight, with the result that I am considered iron-hearted.'

B eyle finished his best-known novels in the way that a child, writing out a sentence and suddenly realising that space is running out, crams in the last letters very small and very fast. The narrative of *The Charterhouse of Parma* effectively concludes with the voice of Clelia in darkness: *'Entre ici, ami de mon cœur.'* Fast-forward three years and within the following five pages – a wrap-up – the child of Clelia and Fabrizio dies, Clelia dies, Fabrizio makes a will (sums of money spelled out) and enters the Charterhouse of Parma (a monastery, never previously mentioned) and dies, the Countess Sanseverina dies, the state prospers. *The Red and the Black* concludes with a similar dash to the finishing line: within the two final pages Julien is executed, Mathilde de la Mole kisses his severed head and buries it, marble carvings are ordered from Italy at great expense, and Madame de Rênal dies.

More often, Beyle simply threw up his hands. His unfinished works include memoirs, novels, plays, a life of Napoleon . . . His many starts and few finishes were due not to laziness – arguably, once you have written many thousands of words, abandoning that project and switching to another involves more work than just finishing the thing – but to a temperamental reluctance to make the numbers *stack up*, or to render any final account.

Beyle wrote his first novel in his mid-forties and died aged fifty-nine. As soon as he started writing he was running out of time. Anthony Burgess was another late starter who didn't get going until he was in his forties. (Burgess and Beyle: both were very young when their mothers died, and didn't get on with their fathers; both loved music and Italy, both moved restlessly from one abode to another, both were suspected of being spies.) And Bolaño, who started writing fiction in his early forties and died aged fifty; introducing one of the many books of Bolaño's posthumously published work, the Spanish critic Ignacio Echevarría noted that 'All his narratives . . . seem to be governed by a poetics of inconclusiveness.'

Conclusions are a form of tidying-up or housework, not always necessary, especially if you are not expecting guests. When I mentioned to X that I'd seen Beyle in London in 2016, she said that sometime in the 1990s she had seen Roland Barthes on a train to Birmingham – Barthes who died in 1980, leaving on his desk an unfinished essay on Beyle.

B eyle was employed for the last eleven years of his life as French consul in the Italian coastal town of Civitavecchia. His work included keeping records of ships coming in, ships going out, and he lived there for longer than in any place since his childhood in Grenoble. He managed to slip away for at least four of those eleven years, but during the long afternoons and evenings when he contemplated death by boredom in 'this little hole of seven thousand five hundred inhabitants' where 'The women spend their time dreaming of ways to make their husbands give them a hat from France', he must surely have sometimes felt that he had never really left Grenoble, the provincial town he had been so desperate to escape as a teenager.

When Beyle left Grenoble for Paris in 1799 his ambitions were as predictable – as *conventional* – as the austerities he was fleeing: military glory and a wicked love life. (The hopes of people who move in the opposite direction, from a metropolis to the provinces, are also often predictable and conventional: less buzz, less distraction, peace and quiet in which to grow rhubarb or write a novel.) He added a career as a comic dramatist to the list and was even worse at that than the first two. No wonder he sometimes lay awake at night – as he records in *Egotist* – wondering if he was clever or stupid, good or bad. 'I've acted according to my mood, blindly.'

It was a strange life, full of acute angles, dedicated to the Polonius strategy: 'By indirections find directions out.' The wonder is that despite or thanks to the often absurd disguises and evasions it's a life remembered now because it included the writing of two novels embedded in the literary canon (the capital city – he got there!) which Beyle doesn't even mention in his memoirs – for the good reason that those don't get as far as the years in which the novels were written, but even so it feels as if they were incidental, just things that somehow happened to him.

Beyle does little to correct that impression. In *Memoirs of an Egotist*, written in Civitavecchia: 'I regard and have always regarded my works as lottery tickets.' Beyle in his 'Second Attempt at a Preface' to *Love* (which, by his own count, 'found only seventeen readers' in the eleven years after its first publication in 1822): 'I am writing for a mere hundred readers, unfortunate, likeable, charming, unhypocritical, unselfrighteous people whom I wish to please; I know no more than one or two.' Writing for almost no one, then, or for himself – a hobbyist, an amateur. Even though his writing was deeply attentive to the political events of his time and how they coursed through society. Consciously or not, by his insistence that he was writing not for the world and his wife but for 'the Happy Few', Beyle was flattering into existence a self-selecting fan-group of readers. But it suited him to affect this pose – to rely on his writing for a regular income would have made literature mere *trade* – and I recognise it. When I say that around a fifth of the books I have put out as a publisher over the past fifteen years have sold fewer than a hundred copies, and that I have never made a spreadsheet in my life, this too is humblebrag.

I read Beyle and try not to read things *into* him but of course I do, and the things have fluctuated over time. Once, he had the glamour – the fake glamour of a character in a novel, but that was its appeal – of a wide boy from the sticks who wings his way to the big city, where he gossips and dazzles at the fashionable salons before going home to bed with a singer from the Opéra. Now, I see that when he stepped off the coach in Paris there was mud from Grenoble still on his boots. We can't run from our provinces any further than we can from our childhood.

Beyle still excites me because he is the kind of writer I could never be: fluent, improvisatory, no truck with revision. But half a century after I first read him, he makes me uncomfortable in the way that my brother does: I see in him things I don't like in myself. The awkwardness is why it works, this thing we have going. We are stuck with each other. We call each other out. Beyle tells me that I use literature as a means of both taking possession of the world and of keeping it at bay. I tell Beyle that I understand the need for disguise and subterfuge, but these can become just manoeuvres or habits, as calcified as the rules of the game they may be designed to evade. He tells me (and he is not the only one) that I don't know how to articulate my feelings, and that I hide behind quotations from other writers. I tell him that his perception of Italy as the land of sunshine, music, the arts and 'naturalness', while France is all meanness and vanity, is crude: between them there are only a few Alps, traversed by the Simplon road, and both countries have their social conventions, literary conceits and humdrum provincial towns from which the young, some of them, are eager to escape.

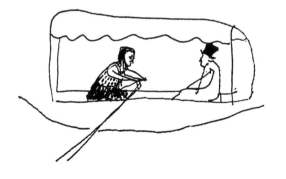

# ℂB *editions*

Founded in 2007, CB editions publishes chiefly short
fiction and poetry, including work in translation.
Books can be ordered from www.cbeditions.com.